The Life, Trial and Hanging of Mary Ball

by

Robert Muscutt

In Coventry in 1849 the author's great, great grandmother was hanged for the murder of her husband Thomas. This is the comprehensively researched account of her life in Nuneaton, her trial, the plea for pardon and finally her execution as the last woman to be publicly executed in Warwickshire.

www.maryball.co.uk

Broadlands Books
www.broadlandsbooks.co.uk

By the same author

Fiction
The Defiance of Mary Ball
ISBN 978-0-9568708-0-3
Broadlands Books
www.broadlandsbooks.co.uk

The Life, Trial and Hanging of Mary Ball

ISBN 978-0-9568708-1-0

Copyright Robert James Muscutt

Cover design: Lars Heilsberger, Solingen

Published Print On Demand by:
Broadlands Books Ltd (Company number: 07556835)

Printed by Lightning Sources UK Ltd, Milton Keynes MK11 3LW UK

Text prepared for POD by Lars Heilsberger, Solingen

Acknowledgements.

Thank you to The Hon Mr Justice Coleridge for his kind permission to use the image of his great, great, great grandfather Justice John Taylor Coleridge by Jane Fortescue Lady Coleridge.
My thanks also go to the Rev Anthony Tooby for permission to use his photo of Mancetter Church.
Thanks to Peter Lee and the Nuneaton and North Warwickshire Family History Society for allowing me to use the image of their Newsletter of April 1999.
We believe the original for our photo of Mary Ann Tonks (Farnell) belongs to the Cook family whom I have been unable to trace for permission to use the image.
All other photos by and with kind permission of Lilian Muscutt (Solingen).

The Life, Trial and Hanging of Mary Ball

by Robert Muscutt

Broadlands Books

Contents

Chapter 1

*

Preview

1849: In the packed, hushed courtroom in the County Hall, Coventry, a woman is standing unsteadily in the dock, outwardly passive and resigned but her mind straining and focussed on the judge seated a few yards away from her. As the judge puts on his black cap, the anguish and tension overcome her restraint. Her body stiffens and she cries out, protesting her innocence and begging for mercy. To stop herself collapsing, she grips the rail in front of her, oblivious to the pain searing through her bandaged hand. The death sentence is inevitable – mandatory in fact – but still his deliberately spoken words strike her like sharp, unexpected blows.

> *"... that you be taken from here to the place whence you came and from there to the place of execution, there to be hanged till your body be dead and afterwards to be buried in the precincts of the jail ... "*

What is she thinking in these moments: of the ultimate separation from her two-year old daughter, the only one of her six children to survive childhood: of the pain of hanging and the unknown horrors of death? Is it rage, regret or simply a protective void that empties her mind, an instinctive response shielding her from otherwise unbearable agony and remorse?

Perhaps she harbours a tiny grain of hope, not the Christian hope of redemption but the commonplace human yearning for some kind of miraculous rescue. If so, it is in vain.

The woman, Mary Ball, was hanged in Coventry on 9th August 1849 for the murder of her husband Thomas.

A scaffold was secured to the exterior prison wall, adjoining the County Hall, where the trial had taken place. The gallows and the trap door though which she plummeted to her death were mounted on the scaffolding and the execution was witnessed by about twenty thousand spectators.

Mary was my great, great grandmother. Her only surviving daughter, also called Mary, was my grandfather Farnell's mother, my mother's grandmother. Despite the years between us, there are only five generations dividing or rather connecting us. That bond is complex and strong. And I'd like to try to tell you the story, the true story, of Mary Ball.

Chapter 2

*

Mary's Childhood and Youth in Nuneaton

FOR most people, especially women, choice is a relatively modern phenomenon. The individual's scope to deviate from the life pattern laid out by society was even more limited in mid-nineteenth century England than it is now. So when we have a general picture of how most young working-class women lived in Nuneaton in the 1820s and 1830s then we have a fairly reliable notion of the main features of Mary Ball's personal life. Work, the constant proximity of illness and sudden death – especially of children, and women giving birth – fear of poverty and the workhouse, these fears were never long out of the thoughts of most working-class families.

Some sought comfort and support in religion and others took refuge in the mindlessness of alcohol. Most gritted their teeth and struggled to make the best of the degradation and suffering that confronted them. Some took part in sporadically organised protest and even insurrection. A few made reckless, individual attempts to change the course of the life mapped out for them. Mary was one of those few.

Fortunately we have the invaluable document entitled *Memorandum Book of Occurences at Nuneaton, commencing with the taking down of the Old Market Cross in the year 1810*, otherwise known as John Astley's Diaries. This painstaking but thoroughly enjoyable record of life in Nuneaton from 1810 until the mid 1840s provides us with a comprehensive and lively portrayal of the town's social, economic and intellectual activity. A few selected extracts give some impressions:

> *29th August 1827: Cricket match played at Hinckley by 11 of the Nuneaton Club and the same number of Hinckley Gents. Was won by Nuneaton Gents with 8 wickets to go down. The novelty of the game in this part of the country attracted 3 or 4000 people on the ground.*

Hinckley 1ˢᵗ Innings   47 – 4 Byes
Nuneaton 1ˢᵗ Innings   60 – 3 Byes
Hinckley 2ⁿᵈ Innings   42 – 3 Byes
Nuneaton 2ⁿᵈ Innings   36 – 0 Byes

Hinckley 96   Nuneaton 99

Nuneaton had 8 wickets to go down

The Stake was £5 aside

Note: The population of Nuneaton at that time was around 6,000. A labourer's wages were about twelve shillings per week. Readers from Hinckley will be pleased to hear that their team won the return match for the same wager on the 12ᵗʰ of September, bowling Nuneaton out in their first innings for 7 runs! In the following year the stakes were raised to £11 per team.

November 1827: Pitched battle (bare knuckle boxing match) *between Abel Vernon and young nudge Green was decided in favour of the former.*

Note: Such fights were illegal but quite frequent, sometimes attracting thousands of spectators and with prize money of £50 and upwards, plus of course any winnings from bets. Abel Vernon was later the constable who arrested Mary Ball!

July 1828: Mr. Joel Bacon destroyed himself in his own chamber by cutting his throat with a penknife. Verdict on the inquest was Lunacy. A collection was made for the widow to amount of about £80.

Note: Suicides were not uncommon. Bankruptcy was one cause. "Lunacy" is probably what we might call severe depression today.

February 1829: Ribbon trade continues bad. The looms not more than half employed since about October last. Prices greatly reduced.

4

October 1830: On the 10th of this month came into operation the Ministerial Acts of throwing the beer trade open and the taking off the whole Beer Duty (about 2/8 per barrel). It excited great interest among the people and was anticipated with no small degree of satisfaction consequently drinking and enjoyment was (sic) the order of the day ...

Note: with typical thoroughness Astley then lists the names of all the *"old Public Houses and the new Beersellers in the parishes of Nuneaton and Coton"*. There were 44 existing pubs and 33 new ones! That makes a total of 77 for a population of about 6,000. The corresponding figures in Hinckley, which had a similar population, were 30 old pubs and 20 new ones after the Act.

November 1831: Ribbon trade worse, Soup shop opened again.

December 1831: The year 1831 was a year of great distress to the dependents on the ribbon trade. Ruin and poverty was the lot of hundreds in this town. The poor rate doubled. 700 gallons of soup were given away weekly.

Note: In November 2,700 people had been receiving *"parochial relief and soup from Charitable Fund"*. Astley had calculated that of a total of 4,219 looms in Nuneaton, 3,482 were unemployed in November 1831.

August 1833: Death of Mr. W. Craddock, said to have died worth £120,000 (one hundred and twenty thousand!). Probably the wealthiest Nuneaton has produced.

Note: Craddock made his money from cheese and corn factoring then property and banking. £120,000 was an immense amount of money; £200 per annum was a decent income for a lower middle-class family: a labourer's wage was about 12 shillings a week.

April 1834: Petitions were agreed upon to be sent to Parliament praying for remission of sentence passed on 6 Dorsetshire Unionist (trade union members).

Note: These unionists were the famous Tolpuddle Martyrs who were sentenced to long terms of transportation and imprisonment for forming a trade union of agricultural labourers, in the words of the judge, "*not for anything they had done but as an example to others*". After a massive public outcry, they were released and repatriated between 1836 and 1838. This entry in the diary, like a number of others, shows that Nuneaton was in touch with national political and social developments.

February 5th 1835: Death of F. Newdigate Esquire of Arbury Hall . . . in his 85th year having possessed the Arbury Estate for 29 years. Said to have died worth half a million (pounds). He was a despicable character – a bad unfeeling landlord – a notorious violator of his word and promises, particularly with his tenants whom he ejected from his farms without mercy. Universally hated as a tyrant ought to be and detested by the honest who knew him of all parties.

Note: Newdigate was of course the employer of George Eliot's father, Robert Evans. A half a million pounds was a vast amount of money, far surpassing even the legacy left by the banker Craddock.

And finally one of my favourite entries, from June 1834 when

". . . a love affair of a romance character occurred at Attleborough, the Hero was a baker whose visit to the Idol of his heart was by the aid of a ladder through her chamber window, as an invitation for which to her person was attached one end of a silk cord the other end permitted to hang down from, the window of her chambers in accordance with preconcerted arrangements. On the occasion which led to the exposure, the ladder was discovered by some women, who removed it, subjecting thereby the fair visitor to effect his retreat in a different direction."

How he escaped we do not know!

In 1818, the year of Mary's birth and christening, cholera epidemics were still unknown in England but even so, infant mortality, especially

6

soon after childbirth, was still very high. Therefore, it is very likely that Mary Ball was only a few weeks old when she was christened as Mary Wright, daughter of Isaac and Alice Wright (born Ward), on 18th June at St Nicolas Church, Nuneaton. About a year later another female baby was christened a few miles away in Chilvers Coton Church, a child who was to become far more famous than Mary and for very different reasons. That girl was Mary Ann (Marian) Evans, daughter of the relatively prosperous manager of the Newdigate estate, Robert Evans, and who was destined to become one of the greatest English novelists under the pseudonym of George Eliot.

There is no evidence that Mary and Marian ever met or even knew of each other's existence, at least not prior to Mary's arrest for murder in May 1849. Yet their lives crossed, whether they knew it or not. They used the same shops, walked the same paths and saw and perhaps spoke with the same people on the muddy streets of Nuneaton in the 1820s and 1830s. Perhaps they sometimes stood together, waiting to be served at Astley's grocery store in the Market Place. Undoubtedly they shared the town's collective experiences in 1832 when sensational events shocked the whole community.

The first cholera epidemics in the UK broke out in 1832, when the disease arrived at the ports probably from India and spread throughout the country. It was not long before it struck with devastating results mainly the impoverished inhabitants of towns like Nuneaton. Abbey Street, then as now the town's main street, was densely populated, packed with overcrowded houses with little or no sanitation. The contaminated water from a shared pump, often polluted by the inhabitants' sewage, was the source of the cholera, though no-one knew this for sure until Dr Snow made his brilliant deductions in London in the late 1840s.

It was in such a house in Abbey Street that Mary Green aka Polly Button lived with her six illegitimate children, and it was nearby that her blood-soaked body was found in February 1832. The nickname derived from her occupation, sewing buttons onto dresses and coats. Let John Astley, the Nuneaton shopkeeper and diarist give the basic facts:

Figure 1: Mary was christened in St Nicolas Church. Thomas was buried in the cemetery there. This was also the Rev Savage's church. It is only a hundred yards or so away from Back Lane.

Feb. 20ᵗʰ A woman named (Mary) Green commonly called Polly Button was found this morning lying in the road in a field ... with her throat horribly cut and was dead. It was not doubted but that the woman was murdered, the situation when found was ab't 22 yards from Mrs Astley's Hovel where it was evident the bloody deed was committed wholly or in part from the large quantities of blood found to be on the straw therein and on the gate of the field in wh. the hovel was in. Groups of people continued to visit the spot on this and several succeeding days. Suspicion fell upon a Farmer's Labouring Carpenter of the name of John Danks who was immediately taken into custody – On Tuesday an inquest was held on the body before Seymour Esq. (Coroner) which was not concluded and was adjourned till the following day when the jury returned a verdict of wilful murder against the Prisoner John Danks who in the course of the evening made a confession in confidence to the Rev'd Mr King, Curate of Nuneaton.

Danks was arrested by Constable Haddon, tried and publicly hanged in Warwick on 9ᵗʰ April the same year. This was clearly an event that gripped the town and the hanging would certainly have attracted huge crowds, especially as the condemned man would be accompanied to Gibbet Hill by a vast procession of spectators.

Astley's store in the Market Place was not only an address for purchasing daily provisions but also for acquiring local gossip, as the diary demonstrates.

In Autumn came the cholera. John Astley's terse diary entries between September and November 1832 convey an eerie sense of the suddenness of the outbreaks and the people's inability to understand the causes.

10ᵗʰ (September) Several cases of Cholera Morbus have appeared in the town, several of them proved fatal, but have been confined hitherto to the more wretched of the population on the Eastern side of the River(Anker).

9

Figure 2: The Market Place as seen from Coventry Street. During the so-called Riots of 1832 the crowd would have spilled into Coventry Street. The mounted soldiers of the Scot Greys thundered into the Market Place along this road.

Oct. 1832 Cholera broke out in a yard in the middle of Abbey Street. Several proved fatal. The Board of Health ordered interment to take place within 12 hours after decease and carried underhand on a bier with as little attendance as possible – the use of a pall was to be dispensed with. Vomiting and purging, coldness of the extremities, cessation of pulse, countenance assuming a bluish appearance, cramps, etc. are the concomitants of this disease.

Apart from the gruelling routine of everyday local life, Mary Ball's Nuneaton also provided a theatre for political drama on a national scale. Towards the end of 1832 the Reform Bill, which extended the franchise to about one in sixteen of the adult male population, finally got through the Lords with the unlikely help of the Duke of Wellington and became law. Together with the accompanying reorganisation of the constituencies, the Reform Bill transformed political life in Nuneaton, as in many other towns and cities. For the first time Birmingham, for example, would have MPs to represent its already sizable population.

The historic excitement of the December election was given additional spice by the presence of Radical candidates who challenged the traditional Whigs and Tories. Nuneaton's Radical candidate was Hemming, the prototype for Harold Transome in George Eliot's novel *Felix Holt the Radical* (1866). The run up to the election is described vividly by the enthusiastically radical Astley. Street parties, banner-waving, bands a-playing and the ringing of bells had heralded the passing of the Reform Bill. Even the nationally famous aeronaut Green had landed his hot-air balloon near Arbury as part of the general jubilation.

When the election proper finally got underway in December, the canvassing included the lavish provision of beer, beef and a whole deer to be roasted and shared out amongst 70 prospective supporters at the Market House Inn. All this indulgence resulted in a boisterous rivalry, but, apart from *"a few electioneering skirmishes (confined to words and gestures)"*, it was free from violence. Unfortunately, this happy, if rowdy state of affairs, was not to last.

11

Figure 3: Another view of The Market Place. Astley's store was in the Market Place, as was Mary's father's pub, the White Hart. The events that form the core of George Eliot's novel Felix Holt the Radical took place here.

George Eliot's novel Felix Holt the Radical describes the fictionalised change of mood.

> "But at present there was no evidence of distinctly mischievous design. There was only evidence that the majority of the crowd were excited with drink, and that their actions could hardly be counted on more than those of oxen and pigs congregated amidst hootings and pushings. The confused deafening shouts, the incidental fighting, the knocking over, pulling and scuffling, seemed to increase every moment. Such of the constables as were mixed with the crowd were quite helpless, and if an official staff was seen above the heads, it moved about fitfully, showing as little sign of a guiding hand as the summit of a buoy on the waves. Doubtless many hurts and bruises had been received, but no-one could know the amount of injuries that were widely scattered.
>
> It was clear no more voting could be done, and the poll was adjourned."

That is, in both fiction and fact, the point at which the trouble really started. The small market town, having been shocked months before by the brutal murder of the immoral but feisty Polly Button, and then decimated by repeated outbreaks of cholera, was in late December about to witness a ruthless demonstration of military power which within a few minutes left several innocent bystanders dead or maimed. It was in some ways Nuneaton's version of the legendary Peterloo massacre in Manchester in 1819. In the midst of the both festive and raucous atmosphere of the polling, the presiding magistrate without recognisable provocation read the Riot Act and our diarist Astley "was surprised to find horse soldiers with drawn swords enter the town, charge upon the people, cutting and trampling down many. One case proved fatal in the day or two after."

Brawling and fist fights on the streets, navvies out on the randy, spending loudly on beer and women at the end of a month's hard work, even the public intimidation of weavers who worked for less than the agreed rate of pay; these were an accepted feature of the rough and tumble life in this crudely vibrant community. But the spectacle of that merciless military precision which left bodies writhing in the mud without any discernable provocation must have terrified anyone who witnessed it. The town had never experienced anything like it and voting was suspended for a day to allow the few privileged with the right to vote to recover from the impact of the atrocity. This was in the Market Place, very close to where Mary lived, so she was very likely present at the riots, as they were later called. According to Marian Evans's widower and biographer John Cross, the future novelist certainly saw it happen, as her vivid descriptions in *Felix Holt* seem to confirm. John Cross states in the biography of his deceased wife that the riot *"was an event to lay hold on the imagination of an impressionable girl of 13"*. He quotes the contemporary report from the local newspaper, which Marian is said to have read aloud to her high Tory father:

"On Friday 21st of December at Nuneaton, from the commencement of the poll until nearly half past two, the Hemmingites occupied the poll; the numerous plumpers for Sir Eardly Wilmot and Mr Dugdale being constantly interrupted in their endeavours to go to the hustings to give an honest and conscientious vote. The magistrates were consequently applied to, and from the representations they received from all parties they were at length induced in aid a military force. A detachment of the Scots Greys accordingly arrived ; but it appearing that that gallant body was not sufficiently strong to put down the turbulent spirit of the mob a reinforcement was considered by the constituted authorities as absolutely necessary. The tumult increased as the detachment of Scots Greys were called in , the Riot Act was read from the windows of the Newdigate Arms; and we regret to add that both W. P. Inge, Esq., and Colonel Newdigate, in the discharge of their magisterial duties, received personal injuries."

14

A plumper was a voter who cast his two votes in favour of a single candidate, rather than splitting his votes. Hemming was the Radical candidate, and Dugdale was Newdigate's favoured man. The local dominance of the much hated landowner Newdigate is clear from this short excerpt. As might be expected Dugdale benefited from the riots and was elected in a constituency where he would probably have otherwise had little chance of success. Not surprising are the great differences between Astley's and the local newspaper's respective reports, as they are at opposite ends of the political spectrum.

Religion and church were major factors in the life of the town, as we know from George Eliot's first work of fiction *Scenes of Clerical Life*, much of which is closely based on real occurrences in Nuneaton in the 1820s and 1830s. Mary was christened, but we know nothing about her to suggest that she was especially religious. Had she held strong religious convictions then she would probably have gravitated to one of the lower church chapels rather than the Church of England St Nicolas Church, which hosted most of the family's ceremonies, such as weddings, burials and Christenings.

It's doubtful that our young Mary travelled much outside Nuneaton or used any form of transport other than her feet. There were not yet any rail links and coaches were expensive. Her life would have consisted mainly of work, either at the family public house at an upstairs loom. Her father's pub, The White Hart in the Market Place, was later reputedly frequented especially by working men who were more politically conscious than the average. In *Amos Barton* George Eliot characterises her home town with her typically uncompromising realism, tinged with compassion:

> *"A flat, ugly district this; depressing enough to look at even on the brightest days. The roads are black with coal dust, the brick houses dingy with smoke; and at that time – the time of the hand-loom weavers – every other cottage had a loom at its window, where you might see a pale, sickly-looking man or woman pressing a narrow chest against a board and doing a sort of tread-mill work with legs and arms. A troublesome district for a clergyman ... for ... the*

miners brought obstreperous animalism, and the weavers an
acrid Radicalism and Dissent. ... and in some alehouse
corners the drink was flavoured by a kind of dingy infidelity,
something like rinsings of Tom Paine in ditch water."

Nuneaton specialised in ribbon weaving, an industry based mainly on home workers, which had been in depression since soon after the end of the Napoleonic Wars. Trade agreements with France allowed cheaper ribbon, a major consumer commodity at the time, to flood the English market. In France, the ribbon weaving industry was technically more advanced than in England, which led to subsistence or even starvation rates of payment for the weavers of Nuneaton. Again, Astley is on hand to provide reliable information on the subject. This extract for 28th September 1829 gives the flavour of the effects of the foreign competition on the militant but raggedly organised weavers.

"During the last week the Town was a scene of Riotous
Tumults. Various outrages were committed on persons by
placing them on an ass face towards the tail and conveying
them in such manner through the streets for having taken
work at low prices. Windows were also broken in several
instances and a general strike for wages ensued. On
the Saturday the Magistrates assembles at Town Hall.
Recommended those who had work to do it and 20 pounds
was left by Mr. Dugdale for distribution to the needy.
However a meeting of the weavers and a few others held this
day when it was decided to discontinue working for a few
days longer hoping to obtain by that time the majority of the
Masters to List Prices. Then to go to work for those Masters
but none to work for less and those without for such refusal
to receive support from the Parish."

By "general strike" Astley of course means general in Nuneaton, not nationally.

A month later at the Warwick Sessions two men were sentenced to two years hard labour and one for six months for their part in "donkeying" the strike breaker.

Just a few miles down the road, between Nuneaton and Coventry, was "Black" Bedworth with its pits and weaving rooms. Especially the mining village Colleycroft was notorious for the unruly and immoral behaviour of its inhabitants. The community, or a part of it, figures in George Eliot's *Felix Holt* as Sproxton. Local history has it that Bedworth was to some extent tamed by the Christian influence of the rector, Henry Bellairs and his family. We shall hear more of the Rev Bellairs later in connection with some recent findings that do not match up with his image of unblemished moral rectitude.

Though very different in many ways to the North Warwickshire where Mary lived, Coventry, about eight miles to the south of Nuneaton, also had its share of poverty and gruelling hardship, as described so vividly in Joseph Gutteridge's autobiography in *Master and Artisan in Victorian England*. Although he was a ribbon weaver who had served his apprenticeship and thus entitled to the freedom of the city, Gutteridge was not spared the destitution rife throughout the trade. This incident, which must have occurred around 1840, provides graphic evidence of the suffering:

An unprecedentedly severe winter set in, and from lack of food and fire we suffered very severely. One night we thought our youngest child was dying from the unavoidable exposure to cold and want, and we had to break up an article of furniture in the dead of night as fuel, to warm the child back to life. For two days not a particle of food had passed our lips, and for nearly a fortnight, in this bitterly cold weather, we had slept on the bare boards huddled together to keep as warm as we could. How bitter my thoughts were no tongue can tell. I was maddened almost to suicide, until the thought of my wife and children would recall me to myself. One morning I stood in front of a baker's shop where the loaves were temptingly exposed, and never in my life was I so near becoming a thief.

Gutteridge, a proud and moral person, resisted this temptation – more out of cowardice than conscience, he says - but his anecdote shows us how desperation drove many into conflict with the law.

Unlike Gutteridge, it is almost certain that Mary had very little schooling or none at all, and that she did not learn to read and write. The Chilvers Coton Free School, now housing the Nuneaton Heritage Centre, was founded by Lady Elizabeth Newdigate in 1753 and extended by her son, Sir Roger Newdigate in the 1770s. In 1834 the school consisted of two large classrooms, one for girls and one for boys. Although there may have been some tuition in basic literacy in some Sunday school classes, the church schools were not founded until 1847 and 1848 in Nuneaton. The Free School was for the poor of the Chilvers Coton Parish, which is not where the Wright family lived. Even more compelling evidence for Mary's illiteracy is the fact that on the existing documents signed by her the signature is a cross, not a name. Current research shows that 44 % of the women who married in 1841 signed the certificate with their mark, indicating they were unable to sign their own name. Mary Ball was almost certainly one of those women who never learned to write her own name. This fact will have a dramatic significance in her story.

As we have seen, life in Nuneaton in the 1820s and 1830s, especially for the poor inhabitants who made up the great majority, was extremely hard and insecure: it was, we could say, pretty grim. To fully grasp that reality today, we have to make a considerable imaginative effort based on the facts we have. But we must also recognise that most people in Nuneaton in general made the best of things and didn't simply resign themselves to the hardships inflicted on them. They suffered but they didn't capitulate. A close reading of Astley's diaries reveals a lively local community fully in touch with the political and social issues unfolding on a national scale.

Let's not forget: the fabric of which Mary Ball's life was a part provided the material for some of the finest English fiction.

Figure 4: Now the much-valued Heritage Centre, this building originally housed the school set up by Lady Elizabeth Newdigate in 1753. It is opposite Chilvers Coton Church, immortalized by George Eliot and where Mary Ann Evans (aka George Eliot) was christened. Her father, Robert Evans, and other family members are buried here.

Chapter 3

*

Marriage

THOMAS Ball and Mary Wright were married on 22nd April 1838 at Mancetter church. Thomas had been christened aged 0 years on 15th May 1821, which made him only 16 or 17 years old on the wedding day, although the marriage certificate gives his age as 20. His bride, Christened on the 28th June 1818, was about three years older. Her given age on the marriage certificate, 21, is also false. And why did they get married in Mancetter, not in the parish where they lived at the time? Thomas's father's occupation is recorded as postman and Mary's father, Isaac Wright, as maltster. One of the witnesses is Thomas's elder sister, Jane Ball, who will have an important role in the unfolding drama of the couple's later life.

The reason for the early marriage and its air of deception is unknown. James Ball, their first child, was christened on January 4th 1839 and died four days later on 8th of January aged 0 years. Assuming the child was not born prematurely, then Mary would have been pregnant on her wedding day, though she may not have known that. There was nothing spectacularly unusual about that, but it suggests that the marriage did not get off to the best start: early pregnancy and death of first child, all within 8 months. Given the age of the partners, we can say with certainty that the marriage started under difficult circumstances. But as we knew from hindsight, things could and did get a lot worse.

On the 1841 census we find Mary and Thomas and their second child William Ball living in Abbey Street next door to or in the same house as Mary's parents and her two sisters, Sarah and Elizabeth aged 14 and 12 respectively. At the same time, on the other side of the River Anker in Back Lane, Ann Bacon (65) was living with her widowed son John (30) and, by all accounts, his younger brother William (10), together with John's own sons John (6) and Reuben (4). John had married Ann White

Figure 5: St Peter's Church, Mancetter, is where Mary and Thomas were married. It is puzzling why they married here and not in St Nicolas.

in 1829, only to see her die in 1837. On 17th September 1843 John Bacon married for the second time. His new bride was Jane Ball, older sister of Thomas. It would almost certainly be after the wedding that Jane moved from her parents' home in Blind Lane into house number 32 in Back Lane with her husband. We don't know exactly when, but Jane and John soon had new neighbours, Jane's younger brother Thomas and his good-looking wife, Mary. So by the mid 1840s the characters who in the course of the next few years formed the relationships and tensions which in 1849 resolved themselves in Thomas's sudden death were living close together in Back Lane. In addition to the married couples, there was John Bacon's younger brother, William Bacon, who was still in his teens when the new residents arrived at some time after 1843. Strangely, young William, or "Flitch" Bacon as he was nicknamed, and who later allegedly became Mary's lover, was probably around the same age Thomas had been when he fathered their first child.

During the trial Will Bacon was confidently referred to as Mary's lover and it does seem extremely likely that the rumor is in fact true. In evidence given at Mary's trial it was said that she got to know her young lover when he was helping out in John Bacon's shop, where Thomas also worked at that time.

Back Lane certainly provided improved accommodation compared with the overpopulated and cholera-stricken Abbey Street. Hardly salubrious, the houses in Back Lane survived until the 1960s, when they were demolished to make way for the new road which by-passes the town centre behind today's library. Ironically the road, Vicarage Street, boasts the new Magistrates Court, very close to the spot where Mary and Tomas were living when the events that resulted in Mary's hanging took place. But in the hungry 1840s Back Lane, though by no means the worst address in Nuneaton, housed mainly weavers' families. The sounds of the looms, clattering into the night, would have mingled with the clucking of hens and the voices of those children lucky enough to snatch time for play. Perhaps some of them sang the song that is said to have arisen on the streets of Nuneaton in 1832:

Figure 6: Ironically the Justice Centre (Nuneaton) now glowers across the road in the direction of where Back Lane used to be.

John Danks played his pranks
On poor Polly Button
To please his wife he drew his knife
And cut her up like mutton.

The fact is that none of Mary's children had yet lived to be old enough to be out playing hop-scotch in the rough road in front of their house.

In twelve years Mary gave birth to six children, only one of whom survived infancy. This was Mary Ann Ball, who was my grandfather's, Thomas Farnell's, mother. Born on 20th January 1847, at the time of her mother's execution Mary Ann was two years old. So at last Mary had a child who was destined to survive. Who knows why this daughter lived when the others had died? Perhaps it was due to an improved environment as the real causes of cholera which regularly decimated parts of Nuneaton, especially the Abbey Street area, between 1832 and the mid century were already being identified. In the1840s Dr John Snow was gathering evidence to support his theory, which he later proved in 1854, that the terrible cholera epidemics were caused by sanitary conditions, especially sewage, and not by *miasma*, as the medical superstition of the day had it. But perhaps the explanation of the child's survival is neither social nor medical but simply human. Sometime after moving into Back Lane Mary probably began an affair with William "Flitch" Bacon. Maybe it was his genes that donated the child with the sturdy constitution that kept her alive until 1927!

We know the marriage was unhappy, especially for Mary. Thomas tried to beat her, went with other women and drank too much. Today, most women in Mary's situation have the possibility of divorce to escape such a marriage and to salvage their lives from the mistake of marrying the wrong person. In 1849 divorce was totally out of the question for a woman like Mary, for practically all women in fact, and for all but very wealthy men. Until 1857 a divorce could require an act of parliament and the grounds on which a woman could file for a divorce were very limited. Adultery in itself was not one of them, though it was for a man seeking to divorce his wife. She might have simply up and left Thomas. But how would she have supported herself? The workhouse and prostitution were the most likely options. Legally, she belonged

Figure 7: On the right hand-side of Vicarage Street, forming a crescent off Bond Gate, is where Back Lane was before the by-pass was constructed. Only a few hundred yards away was the Trent Valley Railway Station.

to her husband as did all her possessions, including, most importantly, her child. Whatever had happened between this married couple, the husband had the right to the custody of their offspring. And now she had the only surviving child of six. Little Mary Ann must have been very precious to her mother. Perhaps she was the real reason why Mary chose a drastic way out of her marriage.

Figure 8: A remarkable image of Mary's only surviving child, Mary Tonks (formerly Farnell). She seems to be in her 70s in the picture.

Chapter 4

*

The Sudden Death of Thomas Ball

O^{N 4}th of May 1849 Mary bought one pennyworth of arsenic from Iliffe's, the local chemist's. As the law required, she and her companion, Elisabeth Richardson, a neighbour, signed for the purchase. There was nothing sinister in buying arsenic, which had many everyday uses in the households of the time; for whitening clothes, for skin care and for killing things – vermin usually. To her sister-in-law's, Jane's disgust, Mary's kitchen was swarming with cockroaches so she bought a decent quantity.

The purchase of the arsenic is described in the report of the trial:

> *"Philip Morris is an assistant to Mr. Iliffe, chemist at Nuneaton; the prisoner (Mary) and last witness (Mrs Richardson) came in and asked for arsenic; he enquired what they wanted it for; they said for bugs; he cautioned them, labeled it 'Arsenic – poison' and they left."*

And again rather more colourfully by Elisabeth Richardson:

> *"she (Mary) asked me if I would go with her to fetch a pennyworth of arsenic. I asked her what for? And she said for the bugs ... I went to Mr. Iliffe's who keeps a druggist's shop; when at the door she said she did not like to ask for it so she gave me the penny to pay for it;... I asked the eldest (of two assistants) for a pennyworth of arsenic and he asked me what it was for and I said the vermin; he gave it to me in two papers sealed up and with big letters on spelling poison."*

At about 9 am on Friday the 18th of May Thomas Ball, after two or three days helping out at Mary's father's pub, The White Hart, during the Nuneaton Fair, met two friends, Joseph Petty and Thomas Watts

Figure 9: On the corner of the Market Place is what was Iliffe's the chemist's, where Mary bought arsenic. Many residents of Nuneaton will remember the chemist's shop.

for a day's fishing in the Little Burton Canal. Unusual for Thomas was that he ate nothing all day and only drank some cold water from a pump. Thomas Watts later testified at the trial that his friend had complained of feeling dry and *"he had had a sup too much at the Fair and his inside was very queer"*.

The men arrived home shortly after 4 pm and Thomas went straight home to bed. We know that Mary was not at home at this time because she later called on Joseph Petty to enquire about Thomas's whereabouts. That must have been between 4 and 6 pm. Watts never saw Thomas alive after they parted at about 4 pm but Joseph Petty, the other fellow angler and life-long friend of Thomas, was visited by Mary in the evening and she told him *"Tom's bad. I want him to have a doctor but he won't."* At 11 the next morning Mary appeared again and urged Petty to go with her to see his friend, who was already in agonizing pain and vomiting heavily. *"Deceased (Thomas) said he could make no water, complained of his belly and being very sick, threw up, and said he should die."* Petty visited Thomas twice more that evening, and on both occasions the dying man was still conscious. During the last visit, at midnight, Thomas complained that his arms were numb and invited Petty to rub them, which he did.

At 2 pm on the 19th Mary went to Dr Prouse with an *"order to attend her husband"*. As a pauper, she needed this for payment of the medical bill. On examining Thomas about half an hour later he found the patient was suffering from intense stomach and bowel pains, was extremely thirsty and the doctor saw him vomit. His diagnosis was "inflammation of the stomach" and he prescribed pills to stop the vomiting. At 7 pm Mary returned to Dr Prouse and begged him to visit Thomas again. After enquiring about symptoms, he refused and said he would call on him the next day. No doubt the minimal payment for a call played some part in this refusal.

At two in the morning of Sunday, Mary called on Petty to tell him that Tom was dead. She had been in an extremely agitated state since her husband's suffering began and when they went back to the body, she had a fit and was unconscious for about 10 minutes. In the morning, Sunday the 20th, Mary came to Dr Prouse to tell him that her husband

Figure 10: The popular bistro The Jail House (Nuneaton) is perhaps on the site of where Mary was held in custody awaiting the outcome of the inquest into her husband's death. From there she was then taken to Coventry Prison. The present building dates from 1896.

was dead. As Prouse testified in court: *"witness (Prouse) gave her a certificate of her husband's death, which was returned by the Constable: it stated that deceased was 27 years of age and that he died of gastritis or inflammation of the stomach."*

Abel Vernon, Nuneaton's second Peelite constable, was a neighbour of Mary's in Back Lane and he visited her on the morning of Thomas's death – presumably after Mary had been to Dr Prouse and received the death certificate from him. Elisabeth Richardson had informed Vernon about the arsenic Mary had purchased. Having also heard all the gossip about Mary's and Thomas's marital problems and the various threats Mary was said to have made on her husband's life, he came straight to the point and asked her about the arsenic she had bought in company of Mrs Richardson. Mary admitted she had bought the poison, for bugs, but had mixed it all in a cup which she had subsequently thrown into Richardson's dirt hole. She had applied the poison with paper, which she later burnt *"for fear the child should get it"*. Like the stubbornly methodical Bobby he was, Vernon searched Richardson's dirt hole on Monday but found no cup. Vernon then visited Mrs Richardson together with his senior Constable Haddon – the same Haddon who had arrested John Danks for the murder of Polly Button in 1832. Mrs Richardson repeated all she knew about the poison and then Vernon went to Mary on the 21st and accused her of giving poison to her husband.

Mary was forced to change her story. She now said that she had not mixed all the arsenic in the cup but had taken out a small quantity and placed it on some sugar-paper which she then laid out on a pantry shelf, where there were also some salts. When Thomas came home ill, he went to pantry to take the salts but must have taken the arsenic by mistake. Unable to account for the whereabouts of the sugar-paper, she was however able to show the policeman a paper with some salts, which she took out from behind an old teapot. Vernon fetched Haddon, who listened to Mary's new story and took her into custody.

Prouse, the doctor who had already certified that Tomas had died of natural causes, now carried out the post mortem. His own findings do not suggest that he was particularly skilled or qualified for the task. He claimed to have found *"white powder"* but he sent a sample of the stomach for examination to someone more competent, Professor of Chemistry George Shaw at Queen's College, University of Birmingham. After carrying out the Marsh Test, Prof. Shaw recovered 3 or 4 grains of arsenic from the stomach sample he had been sent by Prouse. From this quantity which he had found in about a tenth of the stomach, he deduced that there must have been a greater quantity in the whole stomach, far more than would be necessary to have killed Thomas. In a short report in the Coventry Herald of 25 May 1849 the post mortem is referred to and it also reports that:

> *A protracted investigation took place on the Coroner's Inquest on Tuesday (22nd May), which was adjourned till yesterday, and although the issue was confidently anticipated to be a verdict of willful murder against the wife, yet, at the time of our going to press this morning, she had not been committed.*

On the Friday 1st June the same paper noted:

> *On Friday last (25th May) the woman Mary Ball of Nuneaton was delivered over to the custody of the Gaoler in Coventry, to await her trial for the willful murder of Thos. Ball, her husband; having been committed on the warrant of Mr. Jackson, the Deputy Coroner, after the verdict of the jury.*

In the time between Thomas's death and Mary's arrest, she was visited by a neighbour and by her younger sister Elisabeth Wright. There is, however, no mention of Jane Bacon, Mary's sister-in-law and the older sister, who lived next door with her husband John. This sudden lack of contact is hardly surprising, given that Mary was soon to be tried for murdering Jane's younger brother.

Chapter 5

*

The Trial

THE trial took place on 28ᵗʰ July 1849 in the County Hall Summer Assizes in Coventry. The judge was no less than Justice John Taylor Coleridge, nephew of the poet Samuel Taylor Coleridge, and father of the future Lord Chief Justice. His great, great, great grandson is today (2011) a prominent High Court judge, Family Division. Justice Coleridge (1790 – 1876) is described at length by his grandson Lord Coleridge K. C. in his family history *The Story of a Devonshire House* (1906). He was mild-mannered but at the same time a man of intransigent principles:

> *"To those of a later generation his religious views may seem narrow, circumscribed. But they were the views of many of the serious-minded of his age. Religion was part of the core and fabric of his nature ... "*

Coleridge was educated at Eton and at Corpus Christi College Oxford, where he was one of the best students of his day and became close friends with Thomas Arnold, the founder of Rugby School, and John Keble, a conservative high-church Christian scholar and author of the extremely influential The Christian Year. By 1830 Coleridge was a circuit judge and in 1831 was appointed by the Crown to prosecute the so-called Bristol Rioters, participants in disturbances sparked by the failure of the first Reform Bill to become law. One hundred and two prisoners were tried, 81 of whom were convicted. Five were sentenced to death, four of whom were hanged and 1 *respited*, 26 were sentenced to death and transported for life, 1 was transported for 14 years, 6 for 7 years and 3 to various terms of hard labour. This is how Coleridge described the passing of these sentences on men driven to desperate acts primarily by fear for the well-being of their families:

Figure 11: The County Hall, where the trial took place, is in a poor condition today. The brown door is where Mary would have been brought out to be hanged in front of about 20,000 spectators. The side wall on the right was the inside wall of the prison yard.

Today has been the day of reckoning; 5 sentenced to death, and about 18 to transportation for life. I assure you it was a very affecting sight; 3 of the 5 were rude, Herculean fellows, of whom one was in such frightful hysterics that sentence could not be passed for some time. The other two blubbered like women – they were astounded, and I verily believe plunged into the havoc of the riot without any notion of the consequences. The other two ... made no loud demonstrations, but with their heads upon the dock, groaned horribly. Tindal (the presiding judge) *read the sentence; it was very beautiful, but he evidently put such a check on his feelings that he read it tamely.*

After his part in the trials and draconian, merciless sentencing of men whom many today would regard as courageous democrats, Coleridge advanced further in his profession. By the mid-1830s he was very much a part of the Whig Establishment and continued to oppose much reform throughout his life, including in 1857 the Divorce Law, which his friend Keble termed a *"Bill for legalizing adultery"*. Keble published an impassioned plea opposing the reform and Coleridge commented sympathetically on his friend's argument which he describes as *"sound and ingenious"* and which *"display that intimate acquaintance with Scripture which he certainly possessed"*. In fact the 1857 Divorce Act did little more than simplify the administration of the laws governing divorce and left it heavily biased against women. But this was going too far for the judge who was to preside over the trial of Mary Ball.

The trial was one of the cases heard at the Summer Warwickshire Assizes. Judge Coleridge arrived in Coventry around 3 pm on Friday, met briefly with the jury members and adjourned proceedings until 9 am the next day, Saturday 28th July. Mary's was not the only case to be heard. Hers was number 7 on the list and only one day had been planned for all of them. There were two juries present; the Grand Jury consisting of 20 members whose job it was to decide on a majority basis if there was enough evidence for each case to be heard; and the Petty Jury of 12, the dozen men who would decide on Mary's guilt or innocence. The

Figure 12: Justice John Taylor Coleridge presided over Mary's trial, sentenced her to death and also reviewed the plea for mercy for the Home Office. This wonderful portrait belongs to the Honourable Mr Justice Paul Coleridge, who is the great, great, great grandson of the judge in the picture and is himself a high court judge.

only women who played any role in the trial were Mary, her guard and the female witnesses.

The following gentlemen were sworn in as members of the Grand Jury:

Edward Woodcock (Foreman); William G. Sadler, William Ashfort; Thomas Biggs; Thomas W. Blakeway; John Buckley; William H. Butler; William Dugard; Joseph Francis; William Earl; Nevill Low; Joseph Lake (?); Thomas Robinson; Abraham Riley; William Stephenson; Benjamin Walker; David Waters; Thomas Soden; Henry Spencer.

The members of the Petty Jury, the men who reached the verdict on Mar's case, were:

C. P. Walker (Foreman); John Webb; Arthur Starrin; Joseph Peters; Alexander Williamson; John Phillips; William Pickard; John Polley; Samuel Russell; Joseph Robinson; John Sammors; Joseph Ashbourn.

Mr Hayes and Mr Mellor appeared for the prosecution. Their attorney was Mr Craddock. Mary was defended by Messrs Millar and Denison. Her attorney was Mr Cowdell. As the crime Mary was charged with carried the death penalty her legal costs were paid from public funds.

Was it a fair trial? By the standards of the day: Yes. A truly eminent judge of impeccable integrity, jurymen who took their responsibilities seriously and able lawyers all contributed to what must have been seen then as a thorough and balanced trial. The only exception to this was, in my personal opinion, unfortunately the very crucial issue of the jury's verdict: when Justice Coleridge refused to play along with their implicit bargain plea, should they have then defied him and reached a Not Guilty verdict? Perhaps they were swayed by his implication that another instance – a later plea for a pardon – might achieve the leniency they desired and felt to be just. But I hope I will provide enough information for the readers to form their own opinions.

As stated, a thorough trial by the standards of those times, it lasted the whole day, until past eight o'clock in the evening. As the crime Mary was accused of carried the mandatory death penalty, she had legal aid, the lawyers Millar and Denniston, who rightly earned much praise for their work. The prosecution team consisted Messrs Hayes and Mellor. The prosecution strategy was clear: Mary's and Thomas' marriage was an unhappy one and she murdered him to open the way to a new life with her lover William Bacon. The defence lawyers were intent on showing that the evidence on the marriage was simply hearsay and consequently inadmissible. If they could convince the all-male jury that relations between Thomas and Mary were normal, then there would be no credible motive for murder. In the succinct words of the defence team:

"Notwithstanding these quarrels, there was no evidence to warrant the belief that they did not, on the whole, live on good terms together, therefore there was the absence of any adequate motive to the commission of the dreadful crime with which the prisoner was charged."

Selina Ryland, a neighbour, reported that some six weeks before Thomas's death Mary had told her that Thomas had beaten her *"on account of some lies his sister Jane had told him"*. She had cried and added that *"before he should treat her in that way again by heavens she would poison him"*. Later Selina asked Thomas why he had beaten her and he replied that *"he saw enough through the chamber boards with Bill* (Will Bacon)". The only other quarrel she could recall was over an argument about who should fetch a handkerchief – should Mary or should Thomas fetch it himself. Again in conclusion of the row, Mary wished her husband dead, that he should be run over by the first gang wagon that came his way. Failing that fortuitous accident, she would poison him. But this allegedly occurred in *"March or April 1848"*! The defence tried to minimize the importance of these conflicts and the ensuing threats in the able summing up:

"He (Millar) then called their (the jury's) attention to the station of life in which both the prisoner and her husband moved so that they might form a proper estimate of the foul language imputed to her in the course of the quarrels

that had been mentioned. This language did not necessarily imply the existence of feelings more vicious or more vindictive than prevailed in the higher classes of society."

He pointed out that Thomas had admitted he had taken too much to drink during the fair and that *"he felt queer in his inside"* before returning home. This also lent credibility to the supposition that Thomas himself had indeed searched the pantry for salts and taken the arsenic by mistake before Mary returned. Her failure to remove the arsenic from the pantry shelf was attributable to her bad memory, for which there was witness statement. All in all, the defence lawyer claimed the worst that Mary could be accused of was criminal negligence, i.e. manslaughter. In his two and a half hour address, Millar covered all the evidence which incriminated Mary. He concluded:

"By trying the case on its real merits they (the jury) would discharge their duty as reasonable men, which he was sure they would do if they were satisfied without any reasonable doubt. Could they say the woman was guilty? He was sure they would weigh the facts cautiously before they arrived at that conclusion because there would be no remedying such a mistake later in a case of this kind. In cases of a lighter kind there might be a remedy, but in this there would be none."

As reported in the Coventry Standard, Justice Coleridge then summed up for one hour and 25 minutes. He pointed out:

"... the first question for them (the jury) to consider was, whether the prisoner was in possession of the arsenic at the time, on which point he considered there could be no doubt. The next question was, did she administer it to her husband? ... if they were satisfied there was no guilt intention they would return a verdict of not guilty, or if they had the least doubt they would give the prisoner the benefit of it."

After these long statements by the counsels and the judge, the jury consulted for about an hour and a half and returned with a verdict of

41

"*guilty but with a recommendation for mercy*". Pressed by the authority of the Judge to say on what grounds the plea for mercy was based, the foreman replied that they were "*not satisfied with some of the evidence*". In an apparent contradiction of his own clear and correct instructions to the jury before they retired, he now told them that they must retire again to reconsider their verdict. The jury immediately returned a verdict of guilty, whereupon Justice Coleridge pronounced the death penalty.

His closing words were:

> "*Prisoner ... you have been found guilty ... of the horrid crime of murder. The man you accompanied to the altar of God and vowed to cherish, you have ... deprived of life. It is said in the Holy writings, he who sheddeth the blood of man, then his blood shall also be shed ... My sentence is that you be taken from here to the place whence you came and from there to the place of execution, there to be hanged till your body be dead and afterwards to be buried in the precincts of the jail: and may the Lord have mercy on your soul.*"

Clearly for Coleridge this woman had committed a crime not only against man's law but against the Law of God whom she had "*so grossly offended*", against that law which, according to the Judge's deep-rooted convictions, held society together.

Chapter 6

*

The Plea for a Pardon

THANKS to research carried out by Dr Norwood Andrews of Warwick University, we now know that there were two efforts to obtain a pardon or commutation on Mary's behalf. One was a "*Memorial of the Undersigned Inhabitants of Coventry*", a plea by a part of Coventry's Unitarian community based on general arguments against capital punishment. Far weightier was the legally valid document drawn up by Mary's lawyers – "*The Humble Memorial of Mary Ball a prisoner under the sentence of death now lying in Her Majesty's Gaol at Coventry*". In addition, the Rev Savage, vicar at St Nicolas, Mary's parish church, wrote a letter to the Home Secretary Grey, pleading for mercy to be shown. Both Memorials and the letter from Savage are dated 2nd August. On the following day, the 3rd August, the Rev Henry Bellairs, rector at Bedworth, made his own special contribution to the appeal proceedings. Learning of the lawyers' Memorial and clearly knowing something of the contents, he promptly wrote a speedy letter to the Home Secretary of his own: the intention and probable effect of this letter will be discussed later.

Justice Coleridge, the very same judge who had presided over Mary's trial and had sentenced her to death, received the documents from Grey's private secretary, Waddington, and submitted his comments in a four-page letter on 4th August. These were passed on, with remarks of his own, by Waddington to the Home Secretary. Grey's decision to reject the appeals for mercy, was probably made just a few days before the date of execution on the 9th August. The documents were returned by Waddington on the 7th. By any standards, those few days in August were highly dramatic; for Mary they finally slammed the door on any hopes she may have had of mercy.

Let's look closer at the individual documents.

The Memorial signed by John Gordon, Dissenting Minister of Cheylsmore, Coventry, and 13 other men and women was accompanied by a short very self-confident letter addressed to the Right Honourable Sir George Grey, Home Secretary:

> *"Sir,*
>
> *I am invited to forward to you the enclosed Memorial for presentation to her Majesty.*
>
> *It has necessarily been got up in great haste: but if more time could have been allowed a much larger number of signatures would easily have been obtained. A very strong feeling in favour of its object exists amongst the inhabitants of this city."*

The object he refers to is the death penalty rather than Mary herself. The memorial begs Her Majesty to substitute the death penalty with *"a punishment which does not involve the taking away of her life"*. It states explicitly:

> *"Your memorialists do not urge this prayer (for mercy) on grounds peculiar to the case of criminality to which it refers, though they feel that the ignorant and degraded condition of the criminal makes her an object of pity as well as of blame and that her sex increases their natural aversion to so shocking a spectacle as her execution would present."*

The remaining three pages argue in principle against capital punishment on religious, moral and practical grounds and contain no further mention of Mary. It is no surprise that when reviewing the appeals Coleridge paid no attention to this memorial apart from to summarily dismiss its relevance.

The official Memorial submitted by Mary's lawyers on her behalf maintains her innocence *"of the murder of which she lies convicted"*. Almost two full pages, it does have the tight relevance of a legal plea and therefore I quote the list of arguments in full:

44

"That your petitioner is a miserable and forlorn object now lying under sentence of death in the Gaol at Coventry:–

That your Petitioner humbly, earnestly and anxiously saith that she is Not Guilty of the Murder of which she lies convicted:–

That your Petitioner is a Woman of mean Education, defective eyesight, imperfect memory and subject to Epeleptic (sic) fits:–

That your Petitioner is advised that the learned and venerable Judge who presided on the trial of me your miserable Petitioner as far as my distracted memory will afford said:

"That was not the time or place for him to make any observation which might lay the foundation of the hope of mercy."

And that your Petitioner further sheweth that the Jury who passed (judgement) upon the Trial of your Petitioner were greatly divided in opinion, and that they retired and were closeted together for upward of three hours, and that 8 of such Jury were of opinion when they retired from the Jury box in Court that your humble and miserable Petitioner was Not Guilty and to the last and fatal moment the said Jury never were agreed to find her Guilty save upon the promise that she should be recommended to mercy and that in the pursuance of such Bargain your Petitioner was as she is advised improperly and unconstitutionally convicted of an offence of which she now most solemnly asseverates her innocence."

Consequently she implores the Home Secretary *"to think me (miserable tho' I be) a fit subject for the extension of the Royal Clemency"*.

As we have already seen Mary's eyesight and memory both had a bearing on the trial: the former because she may have more credibly confused the arsenic with the salts had her eyesight been poor: and the latter because what Vernon and Haddon took to be a lie about the disposal of the excess arsenic may well have been a genuine lapse of an imperfect memory. The petition claims that 8 jurymen only agreed to a guilty verdict on condition that a bargain be struck – that she be found guilty of a crime but spared execution. The Memorial makes a powerful case and confirms that, as their performance in the trial demonstrated, Mary's defence lawyers were able men who put all they could into their efforts to save her life.

The Memorial was strengthened by the Rev, Savage's letter on behalf of Mary. From David Paterson's research into St Nicolas Church, we know that the Rev Savage was a reforming vicar who strove to make the church's influence on the population of Nuneaton stronger and more positive. Although she lived in his parish, we don't know for sure how well he knew Mary personally but his letter shows he was well informed about the case. He points out that the jury deliberated for two hours before returning a verdict with a plea for mercy: that Mary herself fetched the doctor and showed her anxiety about her husband's health by going to a second medical man when the first refused to attend the dying man, who received 17 hours of medical attention; that Mary had been afflicted with fits from which can be inferred that she was not always conscious of her actions: that her level of intelligence and ignorance also suggest she was not always responsible for her actions. On the basis of these considerations, all of which were mentioned during the trial and supported by some witness testimony, he appeals for a respite to allow investigation which might establish her innocence of any murderous intent. Savage therefore is arguing both inadequate evidence and diminished responsibility as grounds for mercy. It is a compassionate, committed if sometimes haughty plea which persuasively complements the legal strength of the official Memorial.

Now, on the 3rd of August, Coleridge was in possession of the Memorial from the Coventry Unitarians, the official legal Memorial drawn up on Mary's behalf and signed with her mark, and the Rev Savage's personal but forcefully argued plea for mercy. It was easy for Coleridge to dismiss the first memorial as it was on its own admission

46

not related to Mary's case, but the other two carried more weight; one by virtue of its legal validity and the other on the authority of the applicant, a man of the Church appointed by none less than Sir Robert Peel, the Prime Minister of the day.

What was the response of this learned judge, whose uncle, the poet Samuel Taylor Coleridge, had been one of the most respected sages of his age until he fell victim to opium, and whose son John Duke (Baron) Coleridge (1820 – 1894) was later to hold the highest judicial office in the land, that of Lord Chief Justice?

The first sentence of his report sets the tone.

"I do not doubt her guilt at all nor do I see any fact stated by the petitioners that bring it into question."

He then recounts the sequence of events.

"Her husband went out and came home apparently quite well – she reports him ill at about two hours after – and says she wanted him to have a doctor but in fact (that being 6 pm) no doctor was applied to until 2 pm the next day – and he died at 2 am next following. He had been vomiting very much and according to the medical witness had had all the symptoms of laboring under the effect of metallic poison – a portion only of the stomach contents (it might be 1/6th) are examined chemically and a small quantity of arsenic produced – the quantity less material because only a portion of the contents examined and he had been vomiting too much for too long a time."

But the fact that one witness had testified that Thomas had not been feeling well before going home is not mentioned by the Judge. He also implies that Mary was reluctant to call a doctor and that she even deliberately delayed the visit. But is this a fair inference? It was Saturday morning and she would have to get an order from the Parish: Prouse, as the defence had pointed out explicitly in the summary, was one of the *"poor law surgeons (and) had so many persons to attend to*

47

he had no timer to pay this attention (being a pauper) which the case demanded".

A close reading of Coleridge's report conveys the clear impression that he is convinced of Mary's guilt regardless of the jurymen's opinion, who he seems to feel were unduly influenced by some evidence in favour of Mary, or at least by her lawyers' presentation of that evidence. Both during the trial and in his report Coleridge seems to be deliberately steering events, first the jury's decision and now the outcome of the appeal, to an outcome he, not the jury, has deemed desirable. That may, I admit, be unfair to a truly distinguished judge whose integrity and ability are beyond reproach. Readers will form their own opinion.

> *"She was defended by Mellor in a way likely to influence the jury a good deal – some people thought very well – and I was very careful to point everything out to the jury which might prevent their giving undue weight to the statements made by herself.*
>
> *...*
>
> *When the jury gave their recommendation of mercy I asked, as I usually do, on what grounds it rested, telling them that I did not suppose by the question they might not have a good one, but I wished to know it. This evidently embarrassed them much – and one said that some had scarcely thought the evidence strong enough to convict upon. Then I told them they must reconsider their verdict – and in two or three minutes without retiring they found her guilty generally.*
>
> *It seemed to me as the petition now discloses that the recommendation was a bargain. In sentencing her I said something to the effect stated* (in the memorial) *– but added very strong emphasis that I could hold her out no hope – and I saw no reason why mercy should be extended to her."*

The modern reader will inevitably ask why on earth the judge who pronounced the verdict is also dealing with the plea for mercy, especially

Figure 13: The Coventry Cross stands on what was the prison yard. The white wall on the left is the outside of the County Hall and the inside wall of the former prison yard.

as he has already ruled out in principle the remotest possibility that he might change his mind.

But Judge Coleridge was not the final instance in the appeal process. And he was very much aware of his role being restricted to a legal opinion. Therefore his final paragraph is of great importance and shows how very seriously he took his responsibilities. After he has admitted that he was *"compelled to write in haste"* he offers his trial notes to supplement his report and then concludes:

> *"The question, I suggest, as the main one* (whether to grant mercy or not), *must be determined upon principles more familiar to Sir Geo Grey* (the Home Secretary) *& you* (Grey's private secretary, Waddington) *than to me. I cannot say I am at all dissatisfied with the verdict or doubt in any way its correctness – nor do I think such bargains ought to be encouraged – at the same time it is not satisfactory as could be desired in a case of life or death."*

The words *"at the same time"* were tellingly underlined by Coleridge. Though not lending his explicit support to a commutation, the judge is, with his final sentence, making clear that he could accept a show of leniency based on humane rather than strictly legalistic grounds.

When Waddington passed the report on to the Home Secretary, who in effect would decide Mary's fate, there was therefore a hint of hope that her life would be spared. In his accompanying letter, Waddington, having read, in addition to the report, Coleridge's trial notes, concurred with Coleridge's conclusions about the *"propriety of the verdict"* but ended his own brief letter with the words:

> *"... it appears then that both the Judge and the Jury believe them* (the witnesses). *The compromise, then, was a breach of duty on the part of the Jury, and might not, strictly speaking, to have any weight at all on the decision of the case. You will see, however, by the last sentence in Coleridge's letter that he is not quite satisfied.*
>
> *Yours in very great haste."*

As an afterthought, Waddington draws Grey's attention to the fact that *"Thursday next (9th August) is the date of Execution."*

The words *"strictly speaking"* and (not) *"quite satisfied"* are underscored by Waddington to repeat and support Coleridge's emphasis. So, by the time all the documents (the two Memorials, the letter from Savage and Coleridge's report, plus Waddington's short endorsements of the judge's conclusions) were in Grey's possession, it looked as if there was after all some hope for Mary, who had doggedly maintained her innocence in the Coventry gaol.

But there was in the meantime a further, perhaps crucial document available to Grey: a letter dated 3rd August and, as confirmed by the Home Office stamp, *"Received Aug. 4 1849"*, from none other than the Rev Henry Bellairs at Bedworth Rectory. It is certain that Grey read this letter before making his final decision. Perhaps it was the decisive factor in deleting any possibility there had been of a commutation; in other words, it is quite possible that Bellairs' letter ensured that Mary was executed. Before putting the letter into the context of events, let's read it in its entirety:

Sir

The Govnr. of the Coventry Gaol having informed me as one of the visiting Justices of the said gaol that a prisoner under the sentence of death, Mary Ball, had signed a Petition to your Excellency, in which amongst other things it was set forth that her eye sight wanted.

I deem it my duty to acquaint you that any plea for mercy on that ground is false as the Governor of the Gaol assured me that she can read small print without the aid of spectacles.

I beg to add that at the said Prisoner's request I visited her on Wednesday last (1st August) and in consequence of her statement then made to me, I yesterday went to Nuneaton & examined several persons but am sorry to say that I elicited nothing from them which would justify any application by me on her behalf.

This case has naturally created a strong sensation and I was hopeful that I might have been able to address you differently.

I have the honour to be Sir

Your faithful servant

The Rev Henry Bellairs is still something of a legend in Bedworth. There is a school named after him and he features in many stories found in the town's local history and folklore. From 1819 until 1865 he was rector in a rough community consisting mainly of miners and ribbon-weavers. Undoubtedly he had a strong and in many ways positive influence on life in Bedworth: but can we say the same about his role in the efforts to save Mary Ball from hanging?

Mary lived in the parish of the Rev Savage, who as we know made a determined and well-informed attempt to secure evidence of Mary's innocence. Her contact with Bellairs was due to his function as visiting magistrate at Coventry gaol. According to a document we will look at later, Bellairs visited Mary on Tuesday not on Wednesday as he claims. Of course this could be a lapse of memory on the rector's part. Or it could be a mistake made by the journalist who compiled the document in question. The former seems unlikely given the short space of time – maximum three days – between the visit and writing the letter. The latter also seems extremely unlikely as the report is based on the statements of prison staff, who could, if necessary, check the prison visitors books. It also includes the statement by Mary herself that Bellairs visited her on Tuesday. The only other possibility is that Bellairs, to put it harshly, is lying.

It is also more than a little surprising that Bellairs should visit Mary *"at her request"*. He was not the only visiting magistrate at the prison and events a few days later will strongly suggest that he became involved with Mary's case on his own insistence. The prison had its own chaplain and at the nearby St Michael's Cathedral there was the Rev Mr Sandberg who was "unremitting in his attentions" from the time he was appointed to attend her. So why would Mary request a visit from Mr Bellairs? In fact, if, as seems most likely, his first visit took place on the

Tuesday, how could she, so soon after the ordeal of the trial, have found either time or presence of mind to make the alleged request? Perhaps the necessity for this inexplicable, almost impossible haste on her part explains why Bellairs shifted the date of his visit from Tuesday to a slightly more credible Wednesday.

Even more than surprising than his claims about the visit is his unambiguous assertion, based on the alleged testimony of the prison governor, that Mary was able to read small print without the aid of spectacles. Mary's impaired eye sight was an important part of the official Memorial as it substantiated her claim that she had mixed up arsenic and salts. To undermine this evidence was a serious blow to the plea for mercy. What is most remarkable about the claim made by Bellairs is that as far as we know Mary was illiterate. Her marriage certificate of 1838 was signed with her mark, as was even the Memorial presented on her behalf. In that document she is referred to as a woman of *"mean education"*. And in the Coventry Standard's report of the execution it is categorically stated:

> She (Mary) *was 31 years of age. Her father, whose name is Wright, and now keeps the White Hart public House in Nuneaton, ...; he has four daughters, the unfortunate woman being one of them. They were all brought up to the ribbon trade and, as far as we can learn, never received any education.*

Together with what we know about the availability of even the most rudimentary education for girls like Mary in early nineteenth century Nuneaton, this journalistic evidence, which suggests thorough research, shows there can be little if any doubt of her illiteracy. We also know that on Sunday 5th August, the day Bellairs preached the condemned sermon, Mr Stanley, the Governor read to Mary at her request. While this in itself is no proof that Mary couldn't read herself – she enjoyed hearing Stanley read to her – it does further substantiate the other evidence of her illiteracy.

Without questioning the clergyman's veracity, it is therefore hard to explain his statement about her eyesight.

Bellairs visited Mary on Tuesday 31st July or, according to his very questionable version, on Wednesday 1st August. Why? He asserts that he did so *at the said Prisoner's request*. This throws further doubt on the curate's adherence to the truth. In the document already quoted, we read: *"During the trial, and for some days afterwards, she appeared to be indifferent to the awful situation in which she was placed."* And only after Bellairs' second visit did her conduct show *"a change for the better"*. Perhaps on the same day he learned of the official Memorial which was dispatched on the 2nd. Bellairs was resident in Bedworth and in 1849 there was still no rail link connecting Nuneaton, Bedworth and Coventry. So he travelled the ten miles to Coventry and back on horseback or by coach. Then on the following day, the 2nd, he made the six-mile return journey to Nuneaton, where he *"examined several persons."* Who were these *"several persons"*? Surely the person he would have most wanted to consult would have been his colleague, the vicar in Mary's parish. But that person, the Rev Savage, would have furnished Bellairs with information that would, contrary to what he maintained, have justified an application on Mary's behalf. Indeed, as we know, that is exactly what Savage had sent off on the very day that Bellairs was in Nuneaton: an application on Mary's behalf, using evidence that had been corroborated by court testimony.

The blanket statement *"I elicited nothing from them which would justify any application by me on her behalf"* is of course meant to discredit the testimony concerning Mary's epileptic fits and her memory loss, important evidence that Coleridge had also tried to belittle in court. As both a clergyman and Justice of the Peace, Bellairs enjoyed great authority in the estimation of the Home Secretary. With advantage of hindsight, can we share the trust his standing inspired?

So why might Bellairs have committed a double duplicity by falsely claiming both that Mary had requested the visit and then also misleading the Home Secretary about the date? I suspect the explanation is partly to be found in this minister's domineering and self-opinionated character. There is certainly something of what we today colloquially call 'control freak' about the energetic rector. It is generally accepted that the character Mr Fellowes in George Eliot's

Amos Barton is based on the Rev Bellairs. This is how she describes him:

> *At the other end of the table, ..., sits Mr Fellowes, rector and magistrate, a man of imposing appearance with a mellifluous voice and the readiest of tongues. Mr Fellowes once obtained a living by the persuasive charms of his conversation, and the fluency with which he interpreted the opinions of an obese and stuttering baronet, so as to give that gentleman a very pleasing perception of his own wisdom. Mr Fellowes is a very successful man, and has the highest character everywhere except in his own parish, where, doubtless because his parishioner happen to be quarrelsome people, he is always at fierce feud with a farmer or two a colliery proprietor a grocer, who was once church warden, and a tailor who formerly officiated as clerk.*

Whether the details are factual or not, the terse portrayal, for all its gentle irony, is of a self-seeking, smooth-talking, cantankerous sycophant.

Mary's lawyers would have begun as soon as possible with the drafting of the Memorial. We know it was completed by 2nd August at the very latest and Monday 30th or Tuesday 31st are even more likely dates. They would know the whole process would have to be finalised within ten days. The Royal Clemency was ultimately the prerogative of the monarch, Queen Victoria, who from 2nd to 12th of August was on her famous first visit to Ireland. This might have intensified the lawyers' concern with haste. It's even conceivable that Grey was reluctant to bother the Queen with such matters during the elation of her very successful state visit.

So Bellairs somehow gets wind of the fact that the lawyers are preparing a Memorial; he goes to the prison, not on the prisoner's request but with a view to finding out about the plea and then doing what he can to prevent its success. He speaks with Mary, who is probably still traumatised by the death sentence and hardly registers his presence. But he acquires sufficient information, from her or from others, which determines his further action. On Wednesday he hears that his colleague in Nuneaton, the Reverend Savage, has been approached to write a letter on behalf of his parishioner, Mary Ball, something this charitable minister is only too glad to do. On Thursday, Bellairs, if he is to be believed, travels to Nuneaton with the alleged intention of trying to gather information which might work in Mary's favour. The person who could willingly have provided this testimony was the Rev Savage. In fact Savage wrote his plea for Mary on the very day Bellairs claims to have been in Nuneaton. But Bellairs doesn't visit his colleague. We don't know whom he visited. We don't even know for sure he was there.

However we interpret Bellairs' actions, there remains an important question. Why did he go to all that trouble to sabotage what little chance Mary had of mercy? Why did he go to such lengths to ensure that Mary was hanged and that her only surviving child would be left in the precarious position of being orphaned? We know that the child Mary Ann was taken in and was provided with a home by her Aunt Jane, her deceased father's older sister. But did Bellairs know that? For all he knew, the child may have ended in the workhouse.

Bellairs explains his energetic interference in the case with his sense of duty. It was certainly a sense of Christian duty combined with compassion that motivated the Rev Savage to do what he could to save Mary's life. Can we really believe the same of Bellairs, the rector of the neighbouring parish?

We can only speculate on these questions. But to put it simply my personal impression is that whereas Savage saw mercy as a virtue, Bellairs saw it as a sign of weakness, a signal that might be wrongly interpreted by the turbulent populations of weavers and miners in Nuneaton and Bedworth. In other words, he acted out of deep-rooted, instinctive political and social motives, not out of Christian duty or a love of justice. Like Coleridge, he sensed there was something subversive about a woman, even an apolitical woman like Mary, who was prepared to take her life in her own hands and defy state and church in her bid for freedom. In a nutshell, conservative thinking invested in people like Coleridge and Bellairs felt that Mary in some way posed a threat to their authority. If they were seen to condone Mary's crime in the slightest way, even by a justifiable act of mercy, who knows what other latent forces of protest it might encourage? We recall the words of the judge who imposed the draconian sentences on the Tolpuddle martyrs for having the audacity to form a trade union: not for anything they had done, but as a warning to others. In his research note *Arsenic and the Gallows in Mary Ball's Coventry* (June 2008), Dr Norwood Andrews, Researcher at the Centre for the History of Medicine, University of Warwick, writes that:

> *"The murder trial – in which Mary sat silently while witnesses, advocates, jury and judge established an authoritative version of her actions and their appropriate consequences – reflects various cross-currents, one of which was a then-emerging gendered construction of poisoning, not merely as a familiar type of crime but also as a particular social threat."*

That is, I admit, a view some readers may disagree with. Not open to discuss, however, is Grey's ultimate, unequivocal response to the pleas for mercy:

> *The application on the grounds of objection to capital punishment need not be answered.*
>
> *I see Savage's letter is based on other (points). ...*
>
> *I see no grounds on which I would be justified in recommending a commutation.*

It is significant that he also refers specifically to Savage's letter and even took the trouble to consult Coleridge on the points it raised. No doubt, the letter from Bellairs, both a rector and a magistrate, also made a strong impression on the Home Secretary. For Mary this impression was the final death blow.

Chapter 7

*

Torture and Confession

THE two detailed reports of what we now call the torture and confession of Mary Ball were both originally unearthed by Robert Cook, a direct descendant of Mary. The extract from the Coventry Herald and Observer (17th August 1849) provides an objective but at the same time chilling account of the events we refer to as the torture. On the day when Coleridge passed his comments on to Waddington, the 4th August, the prison chaplain, the Rev Richard Chapman, in the absence of the prison governor, visited Mary in her cell for a second time, intent on extracting from her the admission of guilt and repentance she had until then failed to deliver. Already frustrated and inwardly prepared for a repetition of this resistance, Chapman entered Mary's cell and *"immediately ... called for a lighted candle, which was brought to him. He took the candle in one hand and in the other had hold of the hand of the prisoner Mary Ball, which he held over the candle and asked if she felt it. After a time she snatched her hand away, having previously endeavoured to withdraw it, saying at the same time that she did feel it. The Chaplain asked her what that would be compared to the torments of hell, where her whole frame would be burning for a hundred years."*

The witness, the Assistant Matron Susanna Winter, stated that the painful ordeal lasted two minutes and that Mary's hand was blistered. *"The Chaplain afterwards read some prayers and went away ...."* Apparently unaware of any notion wrong-doing, he merely *"wanted to give her some idea of what the torments of hell were"*.

It is a sign of Mary's yet unbroken defiance that when she complained to the Governor, Mr Stanley, *"She declared she would relate upon the gallows what had happened"*.

Bellairs, as visiting magistrate at the prison, was informed and he called for a hearing to be held on the 7th of August, having already suspended Chapman from his duties until further notice. *"At the same time Mr. Bellairs notified to the Governor his intention to perform the morning duty and preached (sic) the condemned Sermon in the Gaol Chapel on the 5th instant, which he subsequently did."*

The terrible assault on Mary was as shocking then as it is today. The famous London-based magazine Punch carried a short satirical report on the incident on 22nd August 1849, comparing Chapman's cruelty with the worst excesses of the Spanish Inquisition. But, if Chapman was clearly the main culprit, there is also something disturbing about the part played by Bellairs in all this. The visiting magistrate who investigated the complaint subsequently lodged against Chapman was, as we know, Henry Bellairs. After only a day or so after his strenuous efforts to do what he could to ensure Mary's execution, here he was offering the condemned woman his spiritual support.

The hearing confirmed Chapman's suspension from duties as a prison chaplain.

After this incident Mary seems to have become more compliant. It may be, as some reports would lead us to believe, that the words of the various ministers of the church suddenly had an effect on her. Also possible is that she was given an opiate to relieve the pain in her scorched flesh and this subdued her spirit.

Now let's turn to the handbill, also discovered by Robert Cook, whose heading reads: *The Confession of Mary Ball as made to Mr Stanley, Governor of the Gaol, to which is added an account of her Execution.*

It is this document which twice gives Bellairs' first visit to Mary as Tuesday 31st July, not Wednesday 1st August, as he maintains in his letter.

This is what Mary reportedly told the Governor of the Gaol, Mr Stanley, shortly before her execution:

"She said, 'I want to tell you something!' I said, 'What is it Ball?' She answered me, 'I did not like to tell anyone else but you! I told Mr Bellairs, on Tuesday, a lie.' I sad, 'What was that?' She said, 'I told him I knew nothing about it myself, but that is false. I put the arsenic on the mantle shelf, and told him there was some salts on the shelf – he might take

them, they would do him good; but I knew at the time it was not salts, but I thought if he taken (sic) it himself I should not get into any scrape about it, for the people would think he took it in mistake.' I then said to her, 'For God's sake, Ball, what made you do it?' She answered me and said, 'Why, my husband was in the habit of going with other women, and used me so ill; no-one knows what I have suffered, but had I have known as much as I do now I would not have done it, for I would rather have left him and gone to the Workhouse; but I hope God will forgive me.' I asked her 'If any one else knew anything about it!' and she said, 'No one.' I asked her how she came to say anything about salts to her husband? She said, 'He complained he was not very well; I thought I would then tell him there was salts on the shelf, but I knew it was not.'"

Apart from providing strong evidence for the level of local interest Mary's trial and execution created, this *Confession* deserves a careful reading. It contains the apparently verbatim admission of guilt provided above. But, although it does have the ring of authenticity, it poses a number of questions.

She had steadfastly refused to confess not only to the torturer, the Rev Chapman, but even to the apparently well-meaning Rev Bellairs, Rector of Bedworth. Let's assume that Mary believed she was doomed to be hanged within a few days. If she was guilty then there was nothing to be gained from denying her guilt. On the contrary, she had the opportunity to confess and thus achieve some degree of absolution from her sins. Now, the day after she had been physically abused by the prison Chaplain, she by all accounts told the prison governor, not a priest, what had really happened.

We should not, however, forget that the plea for a pardon was still pending when the confession was said to have been made. She only learnt of the plea's failure on 7th of August, two days after she confessed. Now let's assume that she still held on to some slight hope that her life might be spared. The plea for mercy was strong and, as we have seen, came within a whisker of success. It is feasible that her lawyer came for

Figure 14: Mary may have entered St Michael's through this door to hear the condemned sermon preached by the Rev Bellairs on the Sunday before her execution.

reason to hope. Why would she then jeopardize even a slim chance of reprieve by delivering a statement of guilt?

There seems little doubt that Mary had a hand in and welcomed Thomas's untimely death, but is what I just quoted a confession of murder? I don't think so. If we accept this confession at face value, she didn't, as Justice Coleridge put it, *administer* the arsenic. The fact is that Thomas did take the poison by mistake. Admittedly, she directed him to it, but he mixed it into his gruel himself. And let's not forget that Thomas was feeling out of sorts **before** he took the fatal dose. She couldn't have known beforehand he'd come home feeling ill. So perhaps the arsenic happened to be lying there on the mantel piece and she spontaneously took the opportunity that chance offered her. Had she not lied or lied a bit more skillfully, she might well have escaped the death penalty, perhaps punishment altogether.

Figure 15: Above us only sky? This may well have been Mary's last glimpse of life before she fell through the trap door to her death.

Chapter 8

*

The Hanging

EVENTS take their inevitable course and on 9th August Mary is taken from her cell, her arms tied at the elbows and pinioned behind her back. Accompanied by the Governor and guards, she emerges from the Lodge Gate next to the County Hall just as the bells of St Michael's peeled out the hour of ten o'clock, just as they still do today.

The scaffold had been mounted to the outside of the prison wall. With the County Hall on the left, the Lodge Gate was next to it on the right between the hall and the prison wall. On the right of the prison yard is the Holy Trinity Church when we look from St Michael's.

The graveyard, like the streets around the prison, would have been packed. There were spectators even on the roof the cathedral. A contemporary report in the Coventry Herald tells us:

> *"She proceeded up the steps with little assistance, and as far as we could observe uttered no word whilst thus awaiting her end, but with closed eyes and saddened countenance stood motionless while the rope was placed around her neck. In an instant the drop fell and she passed from life."*

The reporter adds that *a subdued thrill of horror appeared to pass over the multitude of sightseers as the fatal bolt was drawn.*

Some accounts say that Mary died instantly. But in 1849 the so-called 'short drop' was still used. This was usually too short a distance to result in instant death – unless the hangman resorted to one of the tricks sometimes employed to ensure a merciful quick death. The body had to be left hanging for an hour to ensure the person was really dead. Most of the crowd remained to watch Mary's corpse being removed from the gallows.

65

Figure 16: Cuckoo Lane is one of the streets that would have been packed with spectators on the day of the hanging.

Chapter 9

*

Postscripts

WILL "Flitch" Bacon, Mary's lover, almost certainly kept a low profile until after the dust had settled, and with good reason. Constable Haddon had specifically asked Mary if anyone else had been involved in the crime, a clear hint at Will's possible involvement, something which Mary denied. That may have saved Will's bacon, so to speak. But Will did return to Back Lane, where he lived for more than 20 years with his wife Elisabeth (born Johnson) whom he married in 1852. In 1901 he was still alive.

The two-year-old Mary Ann Ball was now of course an orphan when her mother died on the gallows. But many years later, after the death of both her first husband, William Farnell and her Aunt Jane who had brought her up and whose brother the child's mother had murdered, Mary Ann married Joseph Tonks in 1890. But unusually, though both her and Joseph's families were living in Nuneaton, she chose to marry in St Michael's Church, Coventry. In those days, the journey from Nuneaton to Coventry still meant extra expense and effort for the couple and guests. But of course it also meant that the wedding took place as near as possible to where the bride's mother had been hanged in 1849, more than forty years previously. We can only wonder what she was thinking when she left the Church that day, glancing across to the spot where the scaffolding had been. Perhaps she laid a bouquet of flowers on the spot where her mother died. We don't know and probably never will. But we can go to where the prison yard used to be and stand on the ground ten feet above exactly where Mary was buried. For the many who have done so and it's a very strange experience. And this is perhaps Mary's legacy: the way her story moves people and make them try to understand why she did what she did.

The interest in Mary Ball, in her crime, trial and execution, survives even today. Certainly the woman's death mask on exhibition in the

Coventry Police Museum contributes to this. The composed, almost serene expression on the attractive, full-lipped face conveys something which bonds with most who see it. Those who know the story perhaps ask themselves what drove this apparently ordinary woman to poison her husband when she knew that detection would mean certain death at the end of the rope. Some will take the short walk from the Museum in Little Park Street to Cuckoo Lane and stand with their backs to where the grounds of the old cathedral, St Michael's used to be, facing the busy little square flanked on one side by the side wall of the Count Hall and on the other by the low graveyard wall of the Holy Trinity Church. If they walk forwards to the elaborate replica of the Coventry Cross they pass into what used to be the exercise yard of the old prison. Of course, that imaginary boundary is exactly where the wall on which the scaffold was mounted used to be. But if they look to their right, they can also imagine where the side wall was, just a few yards short of the grounds of Holy Trinity Church. Let's move over with them, from the Cross to a foot or so inside where the wall was. Now we look down at the cobbled ground below us. This is the spot where, in August 1849, Mary Ball, in accordance with the presiding Justice Coleridge's instructions, was buried. It is a strangely moving experience especially for anyone acquainted with the whole story of the last woman to be publicly hanged in Warwickshire.

Chapter 10

*

Time line

The background

27th June 1817
Thomas Ball and Hannah Leedham married in Nuneaton

13th October 1817
Isaac Wright and Alice Ward married in Nuneaton

28th June 1818
Mary Wright (later Mary Ball) daughter of Isaac and Alice Wright christened in Nuneaton

15th May 1821
Thomas Ball, later Mary's husband, born in Nuneaton to parents Thomas and Hannah Ball

22nd November 1819
Birth of Mary Anne Evans, later known as George Eliot, born at Griff, near Nuneaton

18th February 1832
Mary Green, otherwise known as Polly Button, brutally murdered by John Danks near Abbey Street, Nuneaton. Danks was arrested by Constable Haddon.

09th April 1832
Danks publicly hanged in Coventry for the murder.

21st – 23rd December 1832
First general election after passing of Great Reform Bill. In the ensuing so-called Nuneaton riots, several people killed or injured by troops. The events, almost certainly witnessed by Mary Ball and Mary Anne Evans, dramatized in George Eliot's great novel Felix Holt the Radical.

April 22nd 1838
Mary Wright and Thomas Ball married at Mancetter Church. Both give their ages incorrectly.

20th January 1847
Mary Ann Ball born in Back Lane Nuneaton, daughter and only surviving child of Thomas and Mary Ball

1847
The Trent Valley Railway was fully opened in December, linking London with Manchester via Nuneaton.

12th April 1848
The great Chartist demonstration takes place on Kennington Common, London.

The crime

4th May 1849
Mary Ball buys one pennyworth of arsenic from Illife's chemist's shop in Nuneaton Market Place. Her neighbour, Elisabeth Richardson, signs as witness to the purchase.

18th May
Thomas Ball goes fishing with friends Joseph Petty and Thomas Watts. Returns home, feeling "out of sorts". Eats gruel and goes to bed at 6 pm.

70

19th May

19th May

In the early hours of the morning Thomas is in great pain, refuses to have doctor called.

19th May

Mary acquires order from parish and has Dr Prouse examine Thomas at 2 pm. Later the same day Dr Prouse refuses to visit Thomas again when asked to do so by Mary.

20th May

In the early hours of the morning Thomas dies. Dr Prouse is called that morning and diagnoses death by natural causes – inflammation of the stomach.

21st May

Constable Vernon suspects foul play and interrogates Mary. He wants to know what Mary did with the arsenic she had bought some two weeks earlier. He checks Mary's version, finds contradictions and, together with Constable Haddon, he arrests Mary on suspicion of murder.

22nd May

Post mortem carried out by Dr Prouse, and Professor George Shaw at Birmingham University confirms presence of arsenic in Thomas's stomach. Mary charged with murder and taken to Coventry jail to await trial.

The Trial

28th July 1849

Mary is tried for murder at the County Hall Summer Assizes, Cuckoo Lane Coventry. The Judge is Justice Coleridge. After a trial lasting more than six hours she is eventually found guilty of willful murder and sentenced to death. The Judge orders that she be buried inside the prison yard in unconsecrated ground.

Between trial and execution
Day by day countdown

28   Saturday   Trial

29   Sunday

30   Monday

31   Tuesday   The Rev Bellairs, vicar at Bedworth and visiting magistrate at Coventry Prison visits Mary

01   Wednesday   Bellairs falsely claims to have visited Mary on Wednesday not Tuesday

02   Thursday   Mary visited by her daughter Mary Ann with Mary's sister and mother;
Bellairs visits Nuneaton;
The Rev Savage, rector at St Nikolas Church, Nuneaton – Mary's parish – writes letter on Mary's behalf to Home Secretary;
Memorial submitted on Mary's behalf by her lawyers pleading for a pardon;
Testimonial submitted by citizens of Foleshill against capital punishment

03   Friday   Bellairs visits Mary for the second time in 3 days;
Bellairs writes letter to Home Secretary arguing against a show of mercy for Mary;
Mary 'has something to say' but only to Stanley, the prison governor

04   Saturday   Mary tortured by Chapman, the prison chaplain, but still refuses to confess;
                  Coleridge writes report on the Memorial on Mary's behalf;
                  Waddington passes on report with note

05   Sunday   Chapman suspended provisionally;
                  Stanley reads to Mary;
                  Mary confesses to Stanley;
                  Bellairs preaches Condemnation Sermon on his own insistence

06   Monday   Grey turns down plea for mercy;
                  Mary visited by friends

07   Tuesday   Hearing suspends Chapman permanently from duties as prison chaplain;
                  Plea papers returned to Coleridge;
                  Mary learns of "unsuccessful result of the memorial on her behalf from Mr Cowdel, her solicitor"

08   Wednesday

09   Thursday   **Execution**
                  Mary Ball becomes the last woman to be publicly hanged in Warwickshire. The execution takes place on scaffolding erected against the exterior of the prison wall, adjacent to the County Hall in Cuckoo Lane. Around 20,000 people witnessed the spectacle.

                  Burial
                  Mary ball is buried as stipulated within the confines of the prison, on the right hand edge (next to Trinity Church) of the square where the Coventry Cross now stands.

Figure 17: Mary was buried in unconsecrated ground within the walls of Coventry Prison. These cobblestones now cover her burial place.

Chapter 11

*

Family names in Back Lane 1851 and their parts in the case

THE names are used as many times as they appear on the census for each household. The names in brackets are other persons living in the same household – relations, lodgers or servants.

Taylor, Buckler, Beasley, Bates, Marston, Barratt, Bates, Davis (Merdin), Biggs, Merry (Hewitt), Clamp, Vernon, Bates, Hutt, Copson, Farnell, Bishop (Asley), Kirby, Merry, Astle, Biggs, Wheway, Clarke, Toon (Gratrix), Martson, Bant, Buckler, Dawkins (Garrat), Taeddle, Toon, Woodhouse, Taylor, Brooks, Bacon (Bale = Ball), Pratt, Petty, Winters, Ridgway,Ball, Pelley, Green, Winters, Harrard, Watt, Whitmore, Kelsey, Randle (Wheway), Orobinn (Truswell), Keen, Barnes, Dudley, Jephcote, Phillips, Buckler, Buckler, Buckler, Abbotts, Watton, Flowers, Barnsley, Cooper, Barnsley.

Abel Vernon was the constable who questioned and arrested Mary Ball.

William Farnell (then aged 5) later married Mary Ann Ball, Mary and Thomas's only surviving child.

Mary Bishop gave evidence at the trial.

Jane Bacon was Thomas Ball's sister; John Bacon was the brother of Mary's lover, William Bacon; Mary Ann Bale was in fact Mary Ann Ball, Mary's and Thomas' orphaned daughter.

Joseph Petty went fishing with Thomas Ball on the day Thomas took the poison. He gave evidence at the trial.

Thomas Watts went fishing with Thomas Ball on the day Thomas took the poison.

Chapter 12

*

Mary Ball and George Eliot

WHAT did the great novelist know, if anything, about Mary Ball, her working-class Nuneaton neighbour who was hanged in Coventry in 1849?

We know of course that Mary was living in Back Lane and that Thomas, her husband, in the early hours of the 20th May. Two days later on the 22nd a post mortem is carried out on Thomas' body and the original cause of death "inflammation of the stomach" is changed to arsenic poisoning. On the same day Mary is arrested and taken to Coventry gaol to await trial. On the 28th of July at the Warwick Summer Assizes in the County Hall Coventry Mary is found guilty of murder and is publicly hanged on 9th of August in front of twenty to thirty thousand spectators. The scaffolding was erected onto the outside of the prison yard wall next to the County Hall.

Let me summarise what we know George Eliot or Mary Ann Evan, as she was then, was doing when Mary achieved celebrity status in Nuneaton and later Coventry.

Mary Ann Evans had been living at the family home at Griff since her mother died in 1835. However, in 1841 her father Robert Evans agreed to let his eldest son, Isaac take over Griff for himself and his family. So Robert Evans moved with his daughter to a fine house, Bird Grove, on the Foleshill Road, Foleshill Coventry. It was here that Mary Ann came into contact with and became close friends with the Brays. Charles Bray was a quite wealthy owner of a ribbon factory, radical in his politics with a very active in his love life. His nickname the Don Juan of Coventry says it all. But more important for us is the fact that Charles Bray bought the Coventry Herald in 1846, for which Mary Ann subsequently wrote a number of articles. With the Herald he wanted to fight the Coventry Standard's opposition to his reform plans.

So in the second half of the 1840s we have Mary Ann, intellectually brilliant and a fearless pursuer of truth, living close to and often visiting one of the politically most radical and religiously free-thinking circle of friends in Coventry. And the lion of the group owns a major local newspaper.

In May 1849 Robert Evans was very ill and Mary Ann, despite their fundamental differences of opinion in politics and religion, nursed him attentively. From early May her few letters are concerned almost exclusively with reports of her father's health. On the 31 May he died and was buried at Chilvers Coton Church on 6th June. Less than a week later, on the 12th June, Mary Ann left England with the Brays, Charles and Cara, for a long tour of the Continent.

So what are the chances that Mary Ann would have known anything about the murder case that was the talk of her native town, Nuneaton? There is no mention of Mary Ball in George Haight's monumental Collected Letters of George Eliot or in her journals which survived her later husband's, John Cross's censorship. But at least two reports of the case had appeared in the Coventry Herald in late May, one reporting the post mortem and the other Mary's arrest. Is it likely that Mary Ann would have missed these short but drama-packed articles? I don't think so, especially as they appeared in the newspaper owned by her closest friends and for which she herself wrote articles.

And, of course Mary made local and national news when she was tortured by the prison chaplain, Chapman. This became widely known in Coventry. A handbill gave details of the incident and of the disciplinary action imposed on Chapman. There was even a typically satirical report of the incident in the London Punch magazine. The London Times reported on the trial.

Mary Ann Evans was still touring Europe at this time, only returning to England in March 1850. It was while she was in Geneva that she began to keep her Journal, a detailed account of her everyday life and thoughts. Unfortunately, her widower, John Cross, cut out and destroyed the first 46 pages of this intimate record of her life from 1849 – 1854 while he was preparing his much edited and censored Life of George Eliot after her death in 1880.

In a long letter written from Geneva to Mr and Mrs Charles Bray and Sara Hennell, Cara's sister, on 20th August Mary Ann complains of being starved of books to read and thanks her friends *"for the trouble you have taken about my luggage"*. In the next sentence she writes: *"I shall be particularly glad of the newspaper for I never see anything here except daily French papers ...."* The newspaper she refers to is of course the Coventry *Herald*. In a letter written in reply to the Brays on the 28th August she points out that her boxes of luggage have still not arrived. She is obviously longing to receive them and has been told *"it takes a month to get things from England"*. Later in the same letter she writes: *"I am very much amused with the Coventry gossip – pray tell me as much of it as you can. ... I have received no papers yet and I do not know whether any have been despatched. I assure you the four columns of the Coventry Herald would be as interesting to me as a love-letter."* These letters that have survived reveal Mary Ann's undisguised and intense desire to be kept up to date on life in Coventry in July – August 1849. And of course two events that gripped the city's attention were Mary's trial in the County Hall on 28th July and the execution on 9th August. Between these two dramatic days were the torture incident and also the publication of Mary's co-called confession which she made on 5th August to Mr Stanley, prison governor. I have no hard evidence but it seems unlikely to me that none of Mary Ann's acquaintances would have informed her about these sensational news items, especially, as already noted, she was ravenous for news from home and her closest friends owned Coventry's leading source of local news.

As already mentioned, Mary Ann remained on the continent until well into 1850, but what about her companions, the Brays? As the correspondence between them and Mary Ann shows, they were back home in Foleshill. They had left Switzerland on 25th or 26th July. Cara Bray's Commonplace Book has an entry for 3rd August: "Home!" This means that, on the safe assumption that Charles and Cara travelled together, they would have missed the trial but would have been back in time for the execution.

As we know, a petition for mercy was submitted by Coventry opponents of capital punishment. It was signed by John Gordon (Unitarian minister at Cheylesmore, Coventry), Joseph Cash, A. B. Herbert, Thomas Lissaman, Andrew Atkins, Aaron Liston, John Purcell, John Gulson, Edward H. Delf, Stephen Cragg, Mary Colgreave, Catherine Anne Cragg, A. H. Dunn and Samuel Clark. At the time the signatures were hastily collected, the Brays and Mary Ann Evans were still abroad, otherwise they may well have signed. Several of the petitioners were known personally to Mary Ann and possibly all of them were acquaintances or friends of the Brays. Joseph Cash's son John married Mary Sibree, with whom George Eliot had a life-long friendship, some of it documented in the well-known Kirby letters. Edward H. Delph was an Independent minister. He and his wife are both mentioned in George Eliot's correspondence. We are not concerned here with all the details and extent of this fascinating network of social reformers in which the Brays and their young friend Marian were very involved. But clearly the signatures on the Memorial provide further compelling evidence for my suggestion that the Brays knew of the trial and hanging of Mary Ball and would have mentioned it to Marian Evans in their letters.

One other point seems worth mentioning here. As we know, Charles Bray was a life-long supporter of phrenology with a vast collection of plaster casts of famous and infamous people's heads. He even persuaded young Mary Ann Evans to cut her hair and have a cast made! As we know, the so-called death mask of Mary Ball still exists and can be viewed in the Coventry Police Museum. I wonder if Charles Bray had anything to do with this cast of Mary's face being made. This would belong more to physiognomy than phrenology but he was also interested in that 'science'.

And please allow me one final speculation. Bray's newspaper, The Coventry Herald, reported the trial in great detail. If Mary Ann did in fact read this gripping piece of journalism, did it have any influence on her writing, the trial of Hetty Sorrel in Adam Bede, for example? It is generally accepted that the Guildhall, Coventry provides the setting for the trial scene in Adam Bede. The official Warwickshire County Council web site confidently asserts: *"Hetty's trial is undoubtedly set in St Mary's Guildhall, Coventry."* And the description in Adam Bede certainly puts the matter beyond doubt:

"The place fitted up that day as a court of justice was a grand old hall, now destroyed by fire. The mid-day light that fell on the closed pavement of human heads, was shed through a line of high, pointed windows, variegated with mellow tints of old painted glass. Grim dusty armour hung in high relief in front of the dark oaken gallery at the farther end; and under the broad arch of the great mullioned window opposite was spread a curtain of old tapestry, covered with dim melancholy figures, like a dozing indistinct dream of the past. It was a place that through the rest of the year was haunted with the shadowy memories of old kings and queens, unhappy, discrowned, imprisoned . . . ."

Both the physical features and the historical associations fit perfectly to the Guildhall. And it provides the ideal scenario for the fictional drama. Adam Bede was written less than ten years after the real trial of Mary Ball in the County Hall. Was her reading of the reports of that event present in the great novelist's mind when she penned the witness statements, the jury's verdict and the judge's solemn pronouncement of the death penalty?

Chapter 13

*

Transcription of Coleridge's report to the Home Secretary, Sir George Grey

Home Office note:
Report on the case of Mary Ball
Returned 7th August 1849

Coleridge's Report
Heather Court, Ottery St Mary
6.20 August 1849

Dear Waddington

I have read the papers in Mary Ball's case – I don't doubt her guilt at all nor do I see any fact stated by the petitioners that bring it into question. Her husband went out and came home apparently quite well – she reports him ill at about two hours after – and <u>says</u> she wanted him to have a doctor but in fact (that being 6 pm) no doctor was applied to until 2 pm the next day – and he died at 2 am next following. He had been vomiting very much and according to the medical witness had had all the symptoms of laboring under the effect of metallic poison – apportion only of the stomach contents (it might be $1/6^{th}$) are examined chemically and a small quantity of arsenic produced – the quantity less material because only a portion of the contents examined and he had been vomiting too much for too long a time.

No doubt can exist that he died of arsenic – then the prisoner was possessed of arsenic, which even when she bought, as alleged for a lawful purpose, she spoke about in such a way as to show she was aware of that it might be applied in small quantities. Her declaration of angry

83

threatening against him took that shape also. I mean poisoning was the way in which she had threatened to kill him.

Then the statement she made after death. These varied but generally admitted he had taken arsenic and upon two occasions distinctly stated that she had given it to him.

She was defended by Millar in a way likely to influence the jury a great deal – some people thought very well – and I was careful to point anything out to the jury, which might prevent their giving undue weight to the statements made by herself.

In favour of the petition I know nothing but what helped on the giving of the verdict. When the jury gave their recommendation of mercy I asked, as I usually do, on what ground it rested, telling them that I did not suppose by the question they might not have a good one, but I wanted to know it. This evidently embarrassed them much – and one said that some had scarcely thought the evidence strong enough to convict upon. Then I told them they must reconsider their verdict – and in 2 or 3 minutes without retiring they found her guilty generally.

It seemed to me as the petition now discloses that the recommendation was a bargain. In sentencing her I said something to the effect stated – but added very strong expressions that I could hold her out no hope and saw no reason why mercy should be extended to her. It seems to me that the question principally is whether there be anything unsatisfactory in the manner of giving the verdict as should make it desirable to commute the sentence, especially in the case of poisoning, the most wicked and at times most common mode of committing murder.

I am compelled to write in great haste – and I fear unsatisfactorily. I therefore send my notes, which you had better read. They are quite full and I believe accurate. Please send them back to 26 Park Crescent.

The question, I suggest as the main one, must be determined by principles more familiar to Sir Geo. Grey and you than to me. I cannot say I am at all dissatisfied with the verdict or doubt in any way its correctness – nor do I think such bargains ought to be encouraged. <u>At the same time</u> it is not so satisfactory as could be desired in a case of life and death.

Believe me very truly yours.

J. T. Coleridge

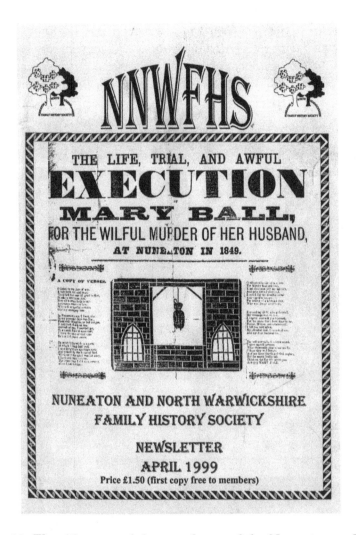

Figure 18: The title page of the newsletter of the Nuneaton and North Warwickshire Family History Society Newsletter (April 1999) which included the author's first article on his great, great grandmother Mary Ball. If you want to read the article, go to www.nnwfhs.org.uk, Publications and click the cover to open the Newsletter.

Chapter 14

*

Post mortem Mary Ball

O NE of my uncles, who until he died in June 2011 at the age of 94, was the oldest surviving direct descendant of both Mary Ball and her husband Thomas, for whose murder she was hanged in 1849. He first heard about his great grandmother's fate in 1949, when the local paper reported on the case on the 100th anniversary. Given that he, like most of his family, had lived all his life in Nuneaton, this collective secrecy, both within the family and neighbourhood, is especially remarkable. After all, his father – Thomas Farnell – was not only Mary Ball's grandson but was given the same name as his murdered grandfather.

I recall knowing something about Mary when I was about 18 (I was born in 1946) but only really became interested in the case in 1998. It was then that I started systematic research. At the time even in local and family history circles in Nuneaton and Coventry, there were few hard facts about Mary. When the results of my investigations were published in the Nuneaton and North Warwickshire Family History Society's (NNWFHS) Newsletter in April 1999 – to coincide with the 150th anniversary – a leading and very helpful member of the NNWFHS admitted she had never previously heard of the case. Another quite well-known local historian in Coventry told me that he had always believed that Mary was a Coventry woman. Of course, Mary was Nuneaton born and bred and probably only went to Coventry for the first time when she was tried and executed there.

A chapter on Mary had been included in each the books *Swing 'em Fair* (David McGrory) and *Warwickshire Murders* (Betty Smith), but both of these informative and readable accounts were based largely on the contemporary reports in the Coventry press of the time. My article established for the first time key data which subsequently provided a basis for further family history research by local genealogists far more skilled and experienced in that area than I am. The most important facts my article recorded were Mary's maiden name, her date of christening and the names of her parents, including their marriage date.

My investigation of the 1851 census also revealed the names of residents in Back Lane, who were involved in the murder – perpetrator, victim, family, witnesses and police.

One question which was invariably asked in conversations about Mary was: what happened to her daughter – her only surviving and suddenly orphaned child? A close look at the Bacon household provided the answer to this question too. In the 1851 census the daughter is listed as Mary Bale (sic) niece, but after comparing the handwriting in other names, it became clear that this in fact was Mary Ball. Further checks put the matter beyond doubt. So little Mary was brought up by her Aunt Jane, the older sister of the man the child's mother had murdered, a scenario no doubt fraught with all kinds of tensions.

This book provides, as far as I know, by far the most comprehensive account of the life, trial and hanging of my great, great grandmother, Mary Ball. While it is amazing how much is now known on the subject, some secrecy, or discretion, in the various strands of the family have certainly concealed, perhaps even destroyed, fascinating insights. What happened to Mary's mother and her sisters after the execution is still today a mystery, for example. Hopefully this book will encourage some readers, especially those directly or indirectly related to Mary and Thomas, to share any evidence they may have, whether in the form of objects, written documents or spoken anecdotes. Our web site: www.maryball.co.uk is also intended to provide a forum for the pool of knowledge and emotions this absorbing history creates.

Thank you for your interest.

Lightning Source UK Ltd.
Milton Keynes UK
UKOW01f0641070318

319006UK00001B/50/P